PROFESSIONAL FASHION ILLUSTRATION RESOURCES

- 40 figure drawing templates
- 4 age groups from 0 to 10 years old
- Multiple pencil illustrations and sketches
- Instructive drawing

Figure drawing templates and fashion illustration by

IRINA V. IVANOVA

Fashion Croquis

FASHION DRAWING: STYLISH AND ACCURATE

With dedication to the loving memory of
our teacher, mother, and friend
Maya F. Rybalkina

Children's Wear Fashion Illustration Resource Book

Children's figure drawing templates with fashion design sketches

by Irina V. Ivanova

Book design by Andre L Milman

Art Design Project, Inc.

Children's wear fashion
illustration resource book:
children's figure drawing templates
with fashion design sketches
by Irina V. Ivanova.

Cover by Andre L. Milman

Editing by Neil Miller

ISBN-13: 978-0692554074
ISBN-10: 0692554076

Book Website
www.fashioncroquis.com
Email: contact@atdesignproject.com

Printed in USA

CONTENTS

About the book
Pages-6-7

Chapter 1
Style Alex
Age group 0-1 years old
Pages-8-33

Chapter 2
Styles Eva and Evan
Age group 1-3 years old
Pages-34-65

Chapter 3
Styles Erica and Eric
Age group 4-6 years old
Pages-66-95

Chapter 4
Styles Jessica and Jess
Age group 7-10 years old
Pages-96-124

Book summary
Pages-125-131

Children's Wear Fashion Illustration Resource Book by Irina V. Ivanova

ABOUT THE BOOK

Who is this book intended for?

This book is created for fashion industry professionals, students and those who want to learn how to draw children's apparel correctly and with style.

What is the main purpose of this book?

The purpose of this book is to make the process of drawing children's wear less stressful and more accurate. Using this book, you can draw children's apparel faster, with better precision, focusing on the creative process of apparel design and not on drawing the body itself.

What makes this book special?

1.   The book is very visual. It is designed to be used as a visual, practical, hands-on guide in the process of illustrating children's apparel. Therefore, by intention, the book contains virtually no text, only some captions. The book is not "about fashion illustration." Instead, it is a practical aid for children's wear illustration drawing.

2.   The book is not intended to be used as a children's wear "style source" or "look book". All garment styles were selected only for purpose of demonstrating the drawing process and do not necessarily reflect current fashion trends.

3.   All illustrations in the book are simple pencil drawing illustrations, created using figure drawing templates from the book itself. These sketches are intentionally left raw, unpolished and unrefined.

4.   Illustrations are depicted with all details, in some cases, showing the step-by-step process of drawing with a figure template.

How to use the book?

Step 1: Select an age group and the pose which fits your project.
Step 2: Trace a figure template.
Step 3: Use your traced template as a back drawing and draw the garment.

What is included in the book?

- 40 figure drawing templates: 10 per each age group.
  Age group 0-1 years old. Style Alex.
  Age group 1-3 years old. Style Eva and Evan.
  Age group 4-6 years old. Style Erica and Eric.
  Age group 7-10 years old. Style Jessica and Jess.

- Each age group includes a template in a static position (still pose) as well as different movements and views (front, back, side, and 3/4).

- Each template is reinforced by analytical lines, aiding to draw garment properly (central lines for arms, legs, and for bodies, waistline, elbow line, knee line, ankle line, side seam line). These lines are very important for fashion illustration. Basic lines will help you to illustrate garment proportionally and symmetrically correct.

- Multiple examples of apparel for each age group are created using templates from the book.

- Analytical visual aid is provided comparing different age groups (see book summary, pages 125-130).

Chapter 1

Style Alex

Drawing children's figure
0 - 1 years old

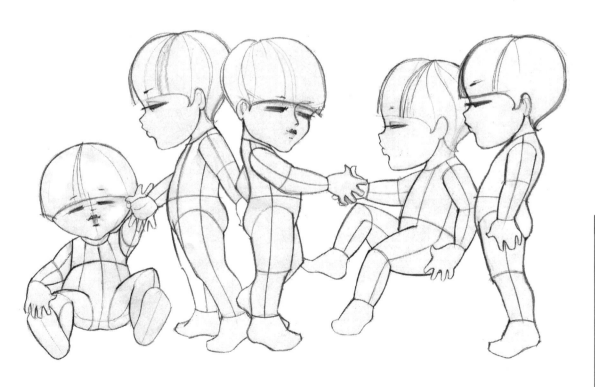

9

Alex

Boys and Girls 0-1 Year Old

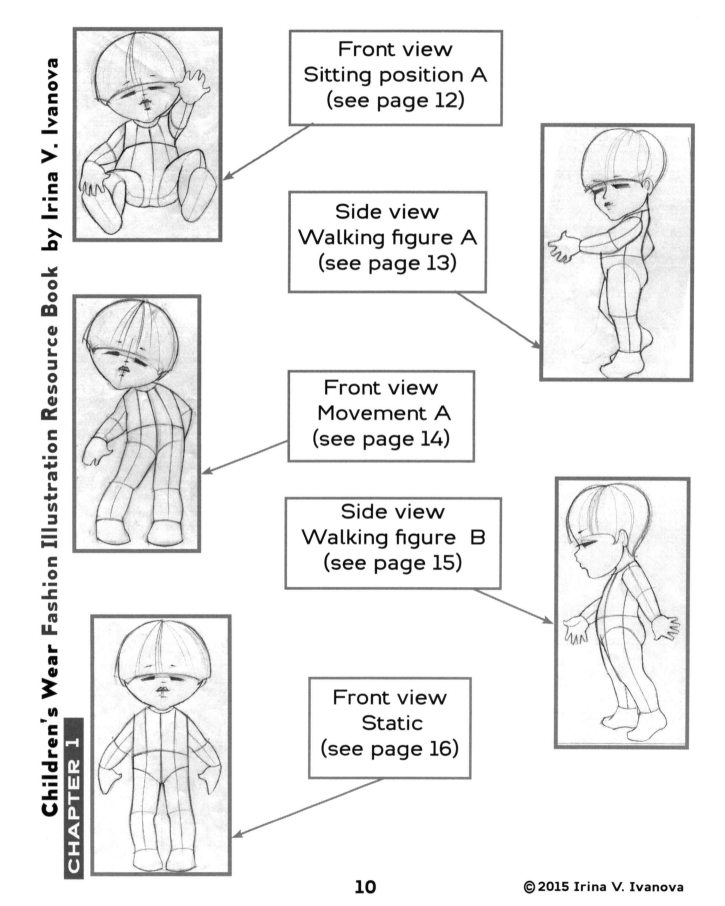

Children's Wear Fashion Illustration Resource Book by Irina V. Ivanova

CHAPTER 1

Front view
Sitting position A
(see page 12)

Side view
Walking figure A
(see page 13)

Front view
Movement A
(see page 14)

Side view
Walking figure B
(see page 15)

Front view
Static
(see page 16)

Alex

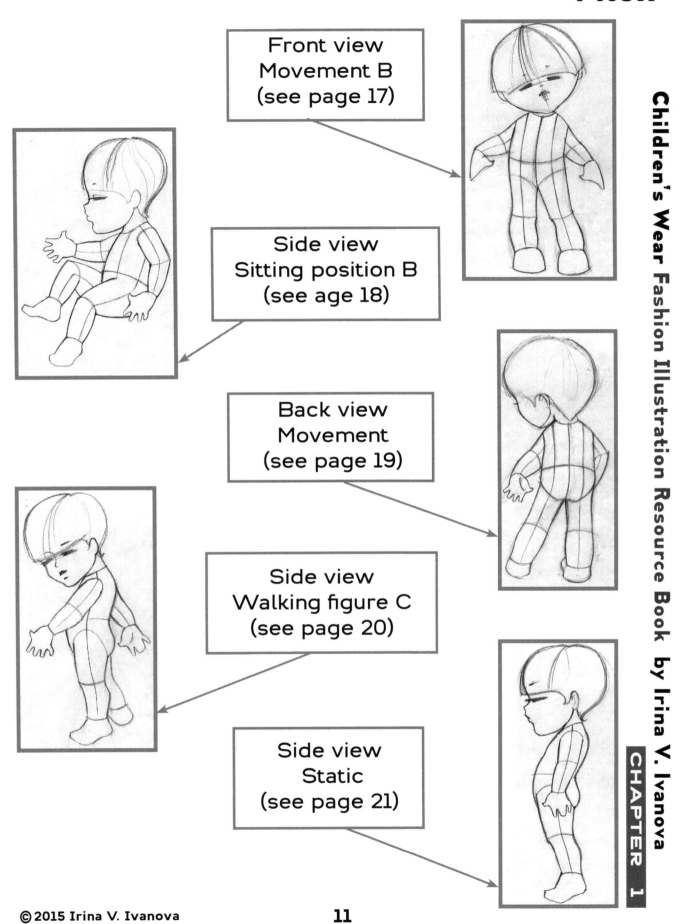

Front view
Movement B
(see page 17)

Side view
Sitting position B
(see age 18)

Back view
Movement
(see page 19)

Side view
Walking figure C
(see page 20)

Side view
Static
(see page 21)

Alex

Front view. Sitting position A

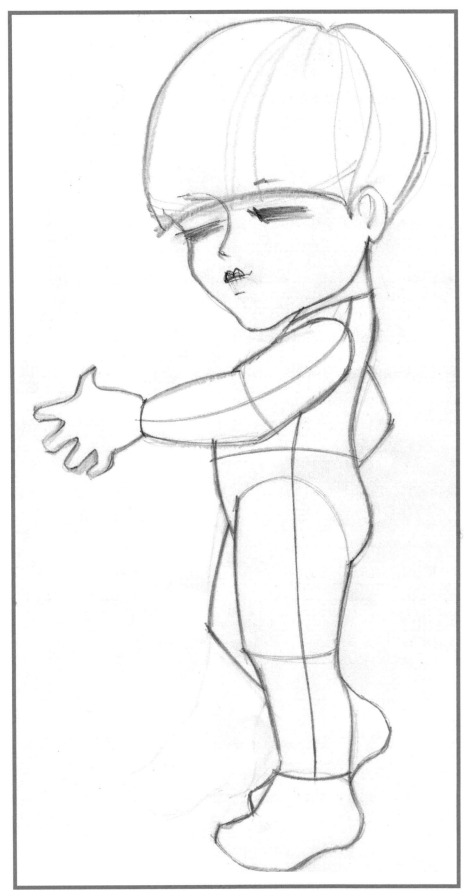

Side view. Walking figure A

Alex

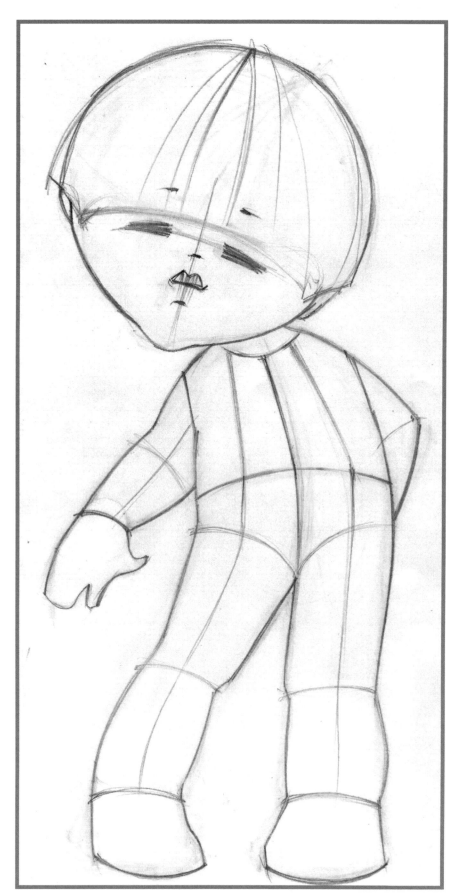

Front view. Movement A

Alex

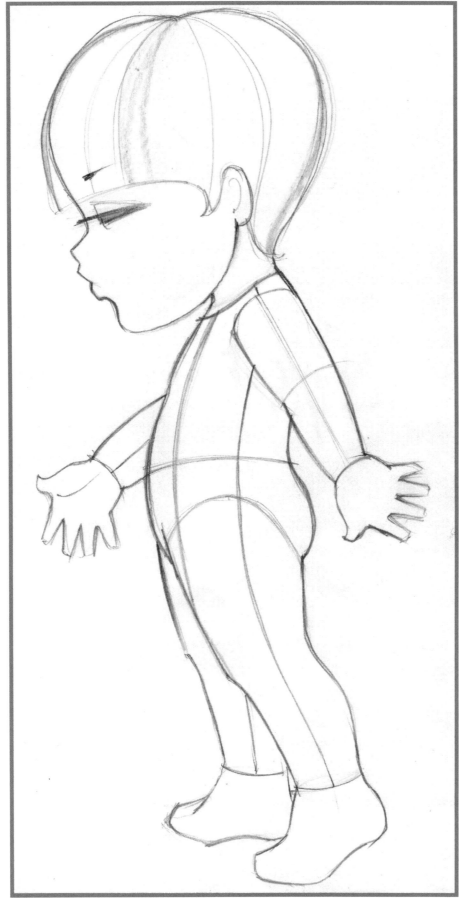

Side view. Walking figure B

Alex

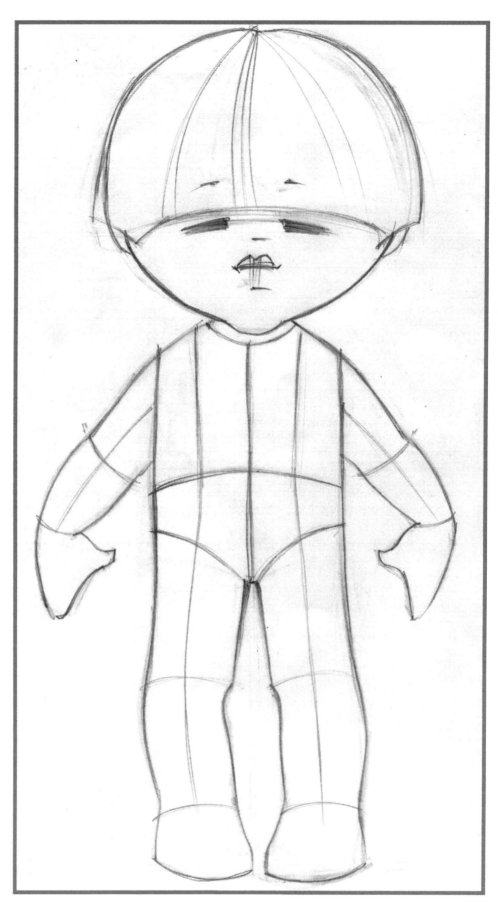

Front view. Static

Alex

Children's Wear Fashion Illustration Resource Book by Irina V. Ivanova

CHAPTER 1

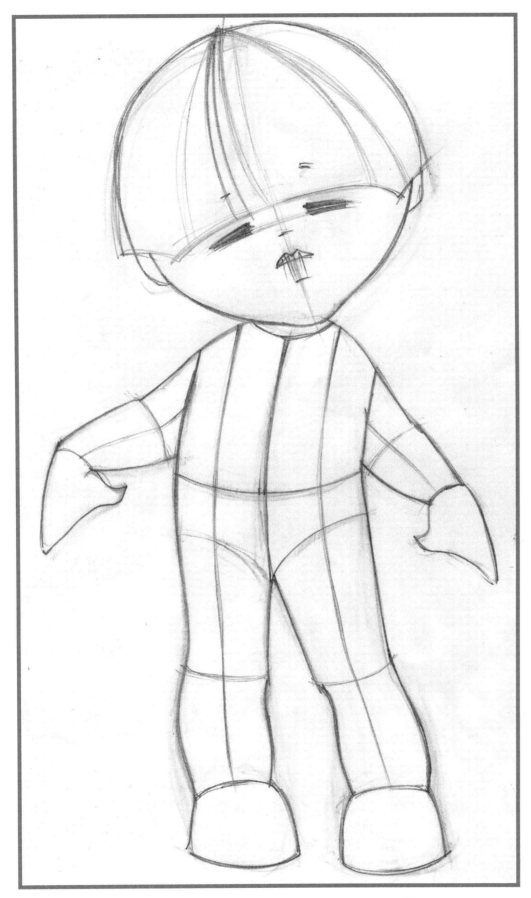

Front view. Movement B

17

Alex

Children's Wear Fashion Illustration Resource Book by Irina V. Ivanova

Side view. Sitting position B

Alex

Back view. Movement

Alex

Children's Wear Fashion Illustration Resource Book by Irina V. Ivanova

Side view. Walking figure C

20

Alex

Panama

Peter Pan collar

Binding for
all edges

IVANOVA

Alex

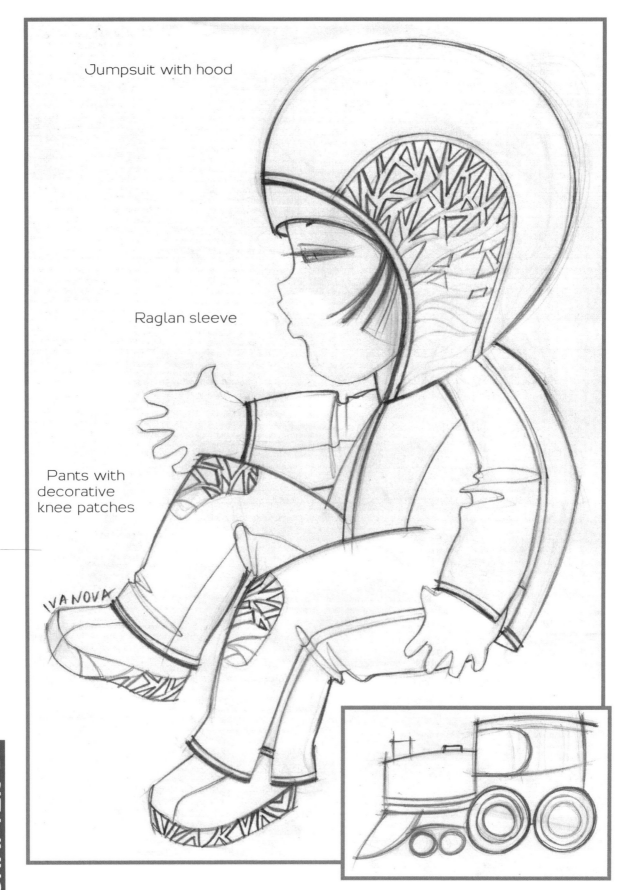

Jumpsuit with hood

Raglan sleeve

Pants with decorative knee patches

26

Alex

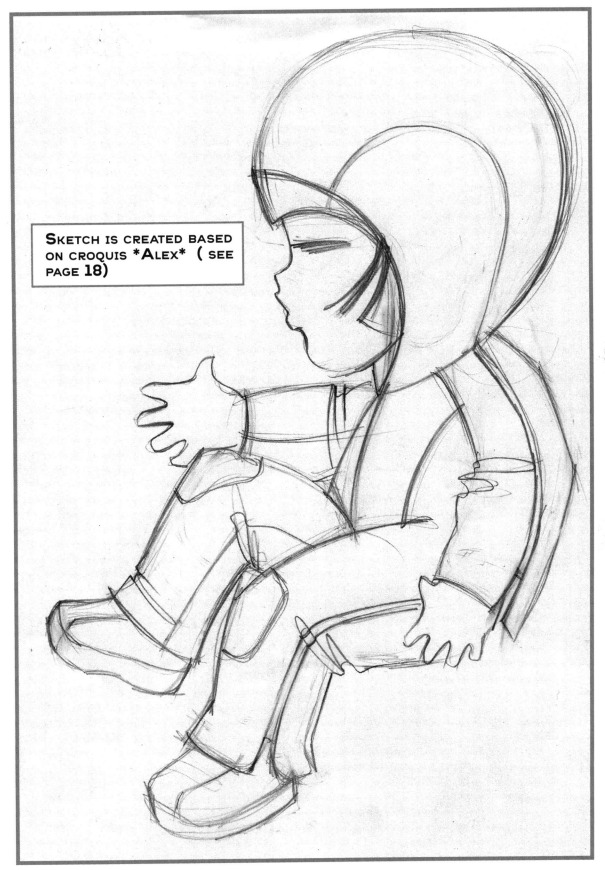

SKETCH IS CREATED BASED ON CROQUIS *ALEX* (SEE PAGE 18)

27

Children's Wear Fashion Illustration Resource Book by Irina V. Ivanova

CHAPTER 1

Alex

SKETCH IS CREATED BASED ON CROQUIS *ALEX* (SEE PAGE 12)

Sleeveless "Sleep 'n play" with built-in feet and V-neckline

Children's Wear Fashion Illustration Resource Book by Irina V. Ivanova

Alex

Children's Wear Fashion Illustration Resource Book by Irina V. Ivanova

CHAPTER 1

Alex

Overalls

Adjustable ties on the shoulders

Binding for all edges

Central panel

Gore

Side panel

Children's Wear Fashion Illustration Resource Book   by Irina V. Ivanova

CHAPTER 1

Alex

Children's Wear Fashion Illustration Resource Book by Irina V. Ivanova

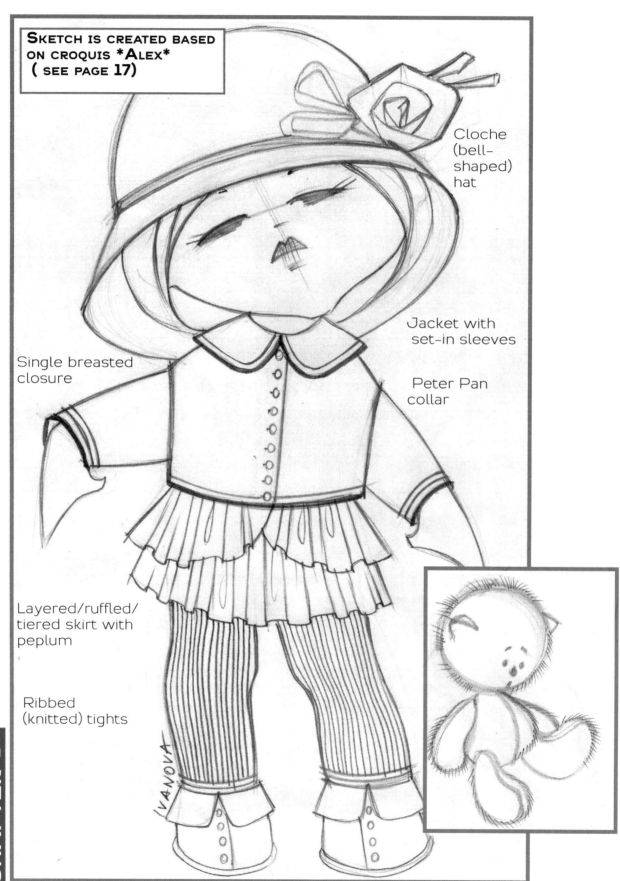

SKETCH IS CREATED BASED ON CROQUIS *ALEX* (SEE PAGE 17)

Cloche (bell-shaped) hat

Jacket with set-in sleeves

Peter Pan collar

Single breasted closure

Layered/ruffled/tiered skirt with peplum

Ribbed (knitted) tights

IVANOVA

Styles Eva and Evan

Drawing children's figure
1 - 3 years old

Eva

Girls 1-3 Years Old

Children's Wear Fashion Illustration Resource Book by Irina V. Ivanova

CHAPTER 2

Side view
Walking figure A
(see page 38)

Side view
Walking figure B
(see page 40)

Front view
Movement
(see page 42)

Front view
Static
(see page 46)

Back view
Movement
(see page 44)

Boys 1-3 Years Old

Evan

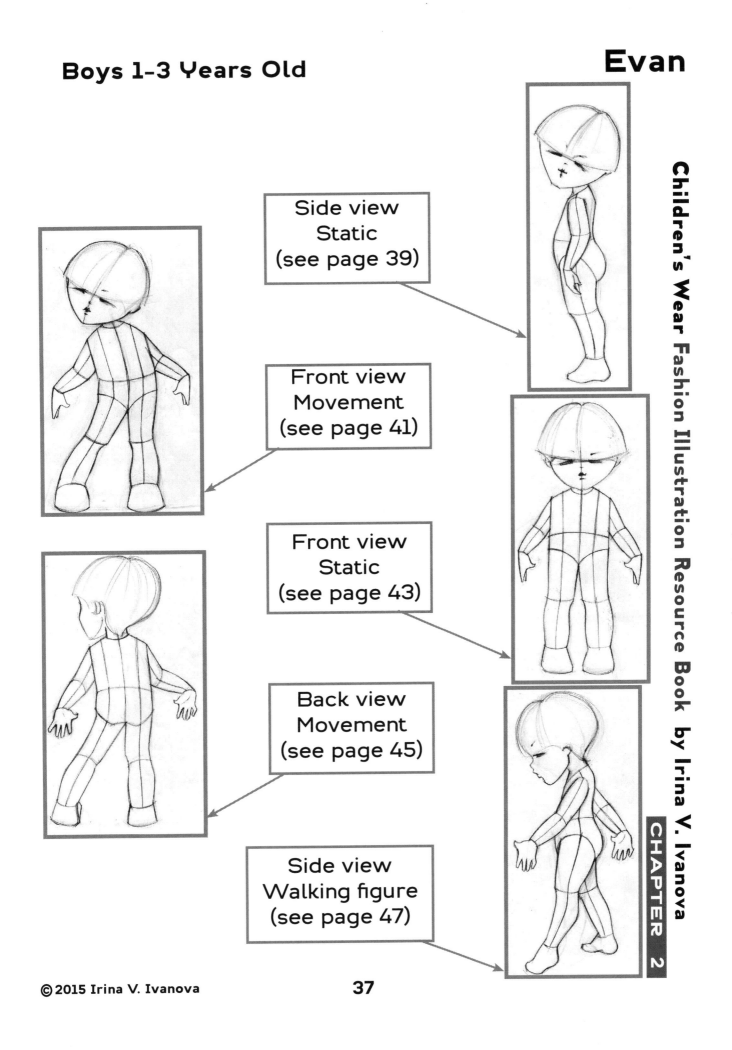

Side view
Static
(see page 39)

Front view
Movement
(see page 41)

Front view
Static
(see page 43)

Back view
Movement
(see page 45)

Side view
Walking figure
(see page 47)

Children's Wear Fashion Illustration Resource Book   by Irina V. Ivanova

CHAPTER 2

Children's Wear Fashion Illustration Resource Book by Irina V. Ivanova

CHAPTER 2

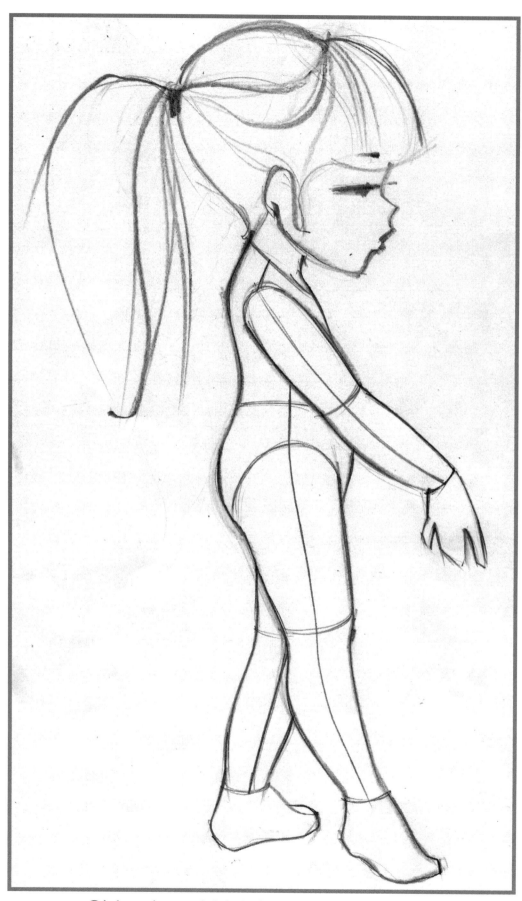

Side view. Walking figure A

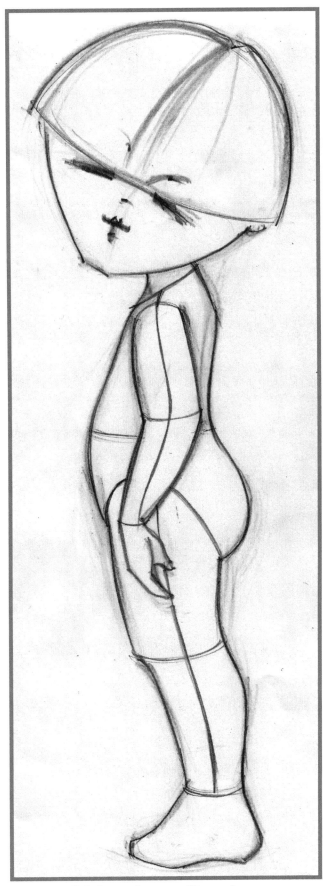

Side view. Static

Side view. Walking figure B

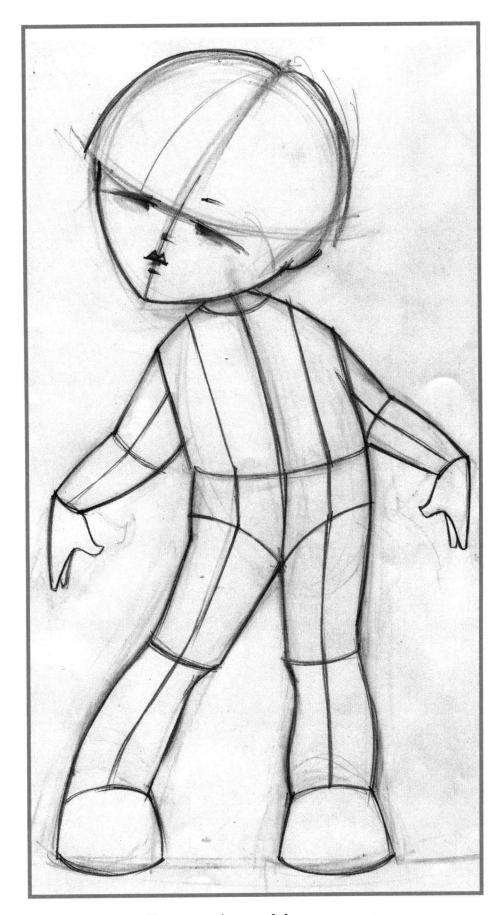

Front view. Movement

Children's Wear Fashion Illustration Resource Book by Irina V. Ivanova

Eva

Front view. Movement

Evan

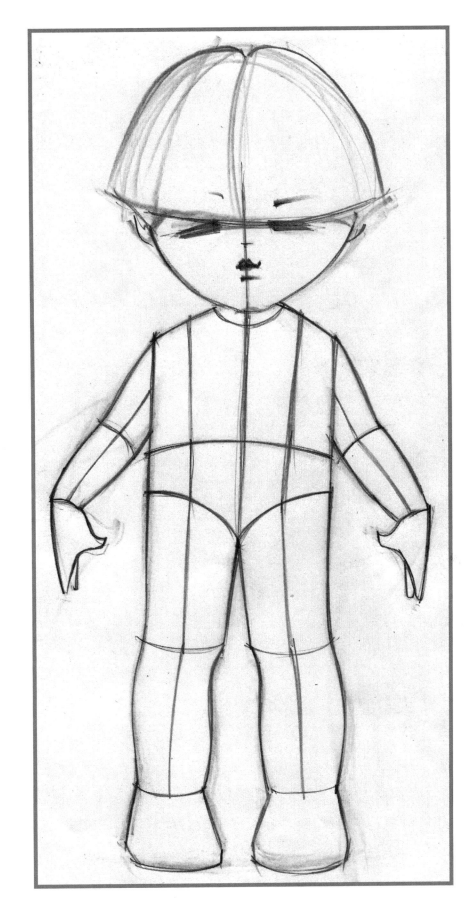

Front view. Static

Eva

Back view. Movement

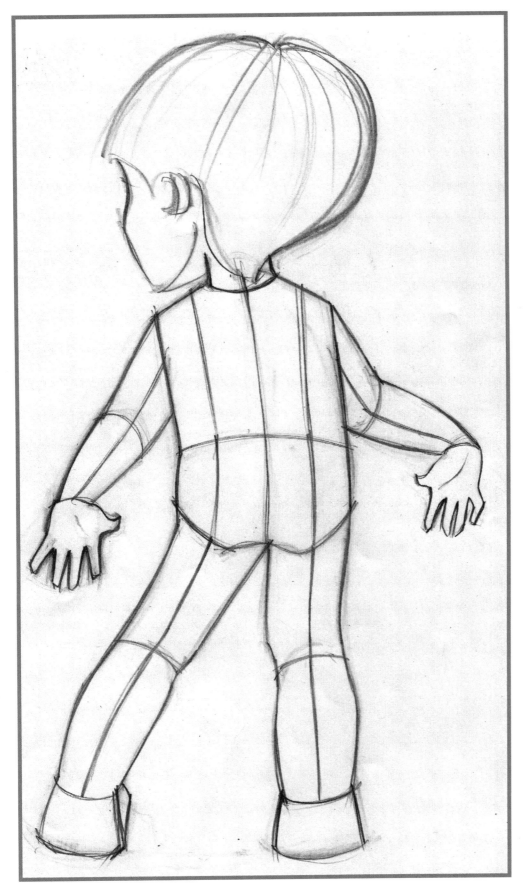

Back view. Movement

Children's Wear Fashion Illustration Resource Book by Irina V. Ivanova

CHAPTER 2

Eva

Children's Wear Fashion Illustration Resource Book   by Irina V. Ivanova

Front view. Static

46

Evan

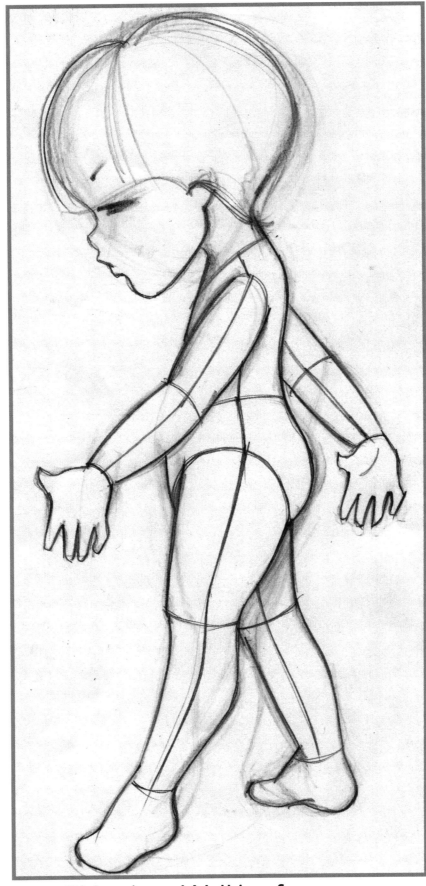

Side view. Walking figure

47

Eva

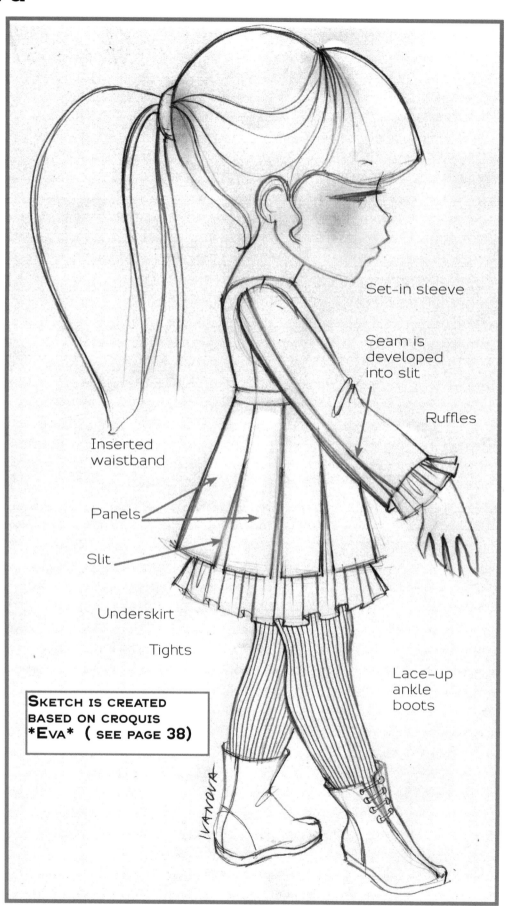

Set-in sleeve

Seam is developed into slit

Ruffles

Inserted waistband

Panels

Slit

Underskirt

Tights

Lace-up ankle boots

SKETCH IS CREATED BASED ON CROQUIS *EVA* (SEE PAGE 38)

Children's Wear Fashion Illustration Resource Book by Irina V. Ivanova

CHAPTER 2

Eva

Children's Wear Fashion Illustration Resource Book   by Irina V. Ivanova

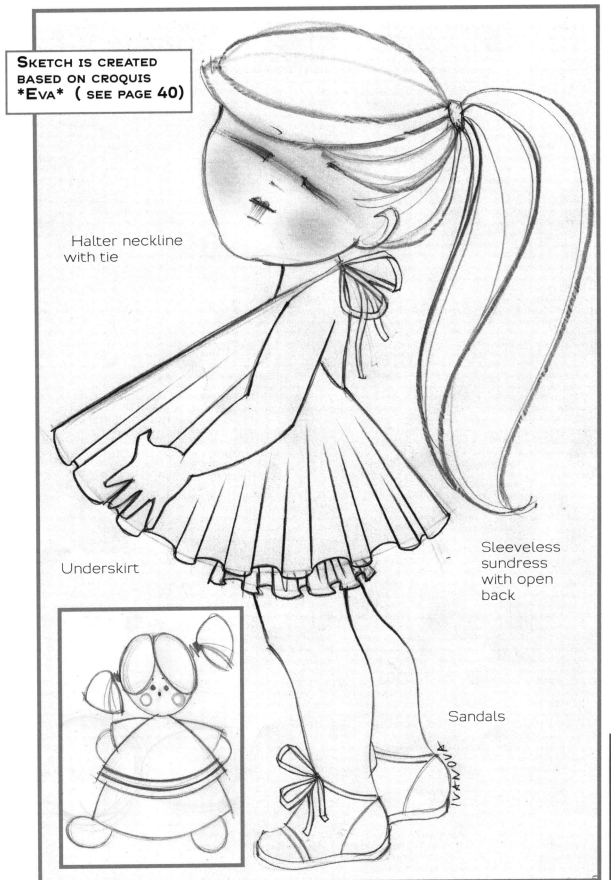

SKETCH IS CREATED BASED ON CROQUIS *EVA* (SEE PAGE 40)

Halter neckline with tie

Underskirt

Sleeveless sundress with open back

Sandals

Evan

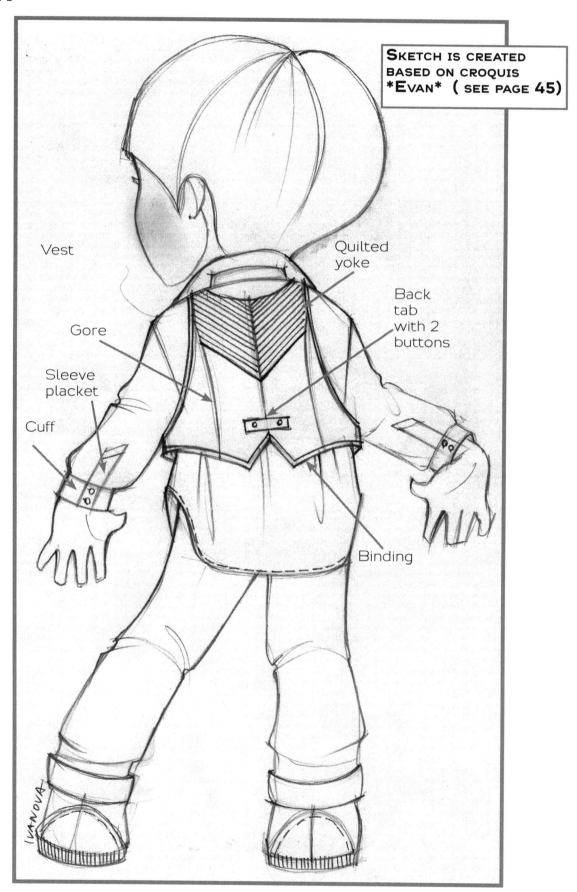

Children's Wear Fashion Illustration Resource Book by Irina V. Ivanova

SKETCH IS CREATED
BASED ON CROQUIS
EVAN (SEE PAGE 45)

Vest

Quilted
yoke

Back
tab
with 2
buttons

Gore

Sleeve
placket

Cuff

Binding

IVANOVA

50

© 2015 Irina V. Ivanova

Evan

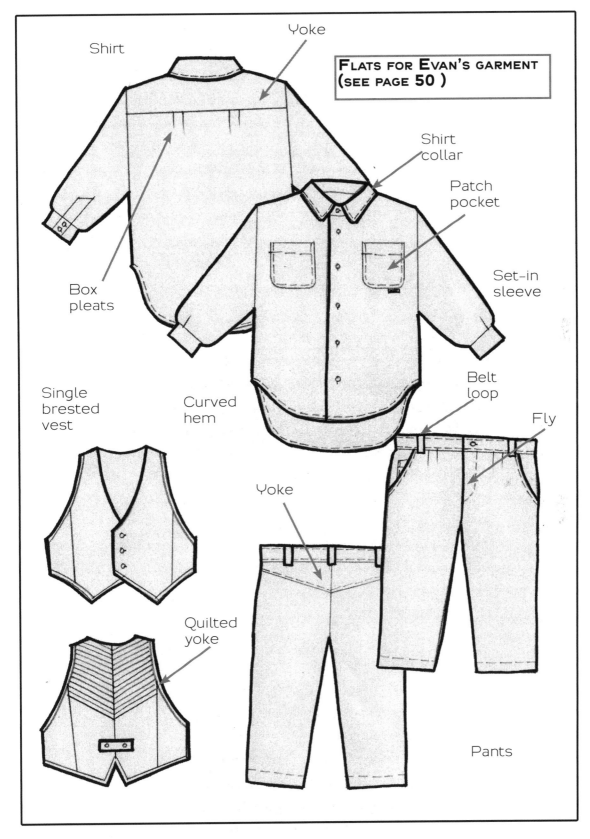

Yoke

Shirt

FLATS FOR EVAN'S GARMENT
(SEE PAGE 50)

Shirt
collar

Patch
pocket

Set-in
sleeve

Box
pleats

Single
brested
vest

Curved
hem

Belt
loop

Fly

Yoke

Quilted
yoke

Pants

Eva and Evan

SKETCHES ARE CREATED BASED ON CROQUIS *EVAN* (SEE PAGE 41) AND *EVA*(SEE PAGE 42)

Children's Wear Fashion Illustration Resource Book by Irina V. Ivanova

Cap

Dropped shoulder (relaxed) set-in sleeve

Patch pocket

lace-up ankle bootie

Panama

One-piece swimsuit

Ruffles

Sandals

IVANOVA

52

A- Silhouette dress

Bow

Set-in sleeves (cap style)

Socks

Side Insert

Overalls

Gore

SKETCHES ARE CREATED BASED ON CROQUIS *EVAN* (SEE PAGE 43) AND *EVA*(SEE PAGE 46)

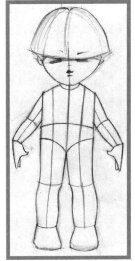

Evan

Children's Wear Fashion Illustration Resource Book by Irina V. Ivanova

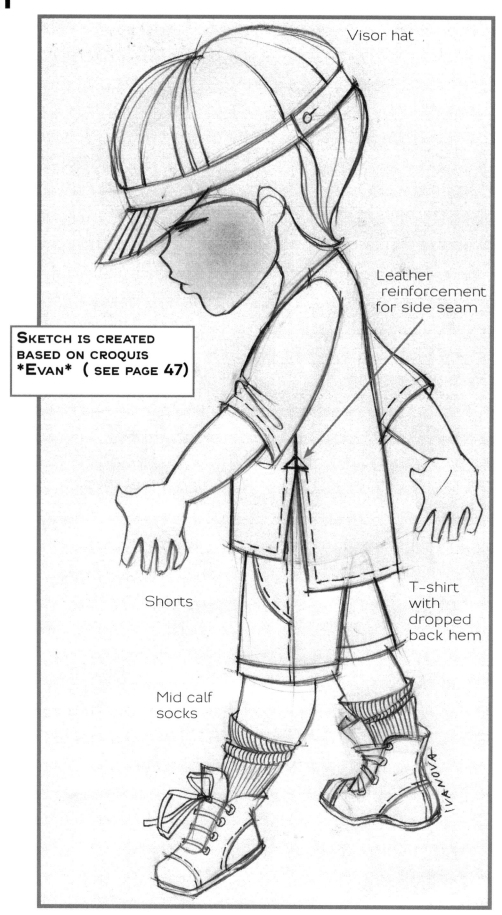

Visor hat

Leather reinforcement for side seam

SKETCH IS CREATED BASED ON CROQUIS *EVAN* (SEE PAGE 47)

Shorts

T-shirt with dropped back hem

Mid calf socks

IVANOVA

Evan

Knitted hat

SKETCH IS CREATED
BASED ON CROQUIS
EVAN (SEE PAGE 39)

Scarf

Dropped
curved
back
hem

Fringing

Side
seam
Insert

IVANOVA

55

Evan

Children's Wear Fashion Illustration Resource Book by Irina V. Ivanova

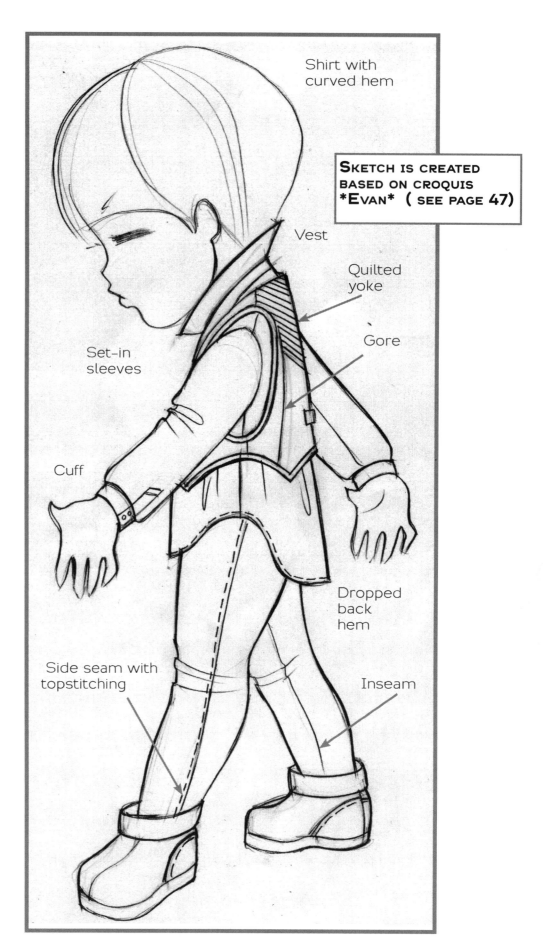

Shirt with curved hem

SKETCH IS CREATED BASED ON CROQUIS *EVAN* (SEE PAGE 47)

Vest

Quilted yoke

Set-in sleeves

Gore

Cuff

Dropped back hem

Side seam with topstitching

Inseam

56

SKETCH IS CREATED
BASED ON CROQUIS
EVA (SEE PAGE 40)

Eva

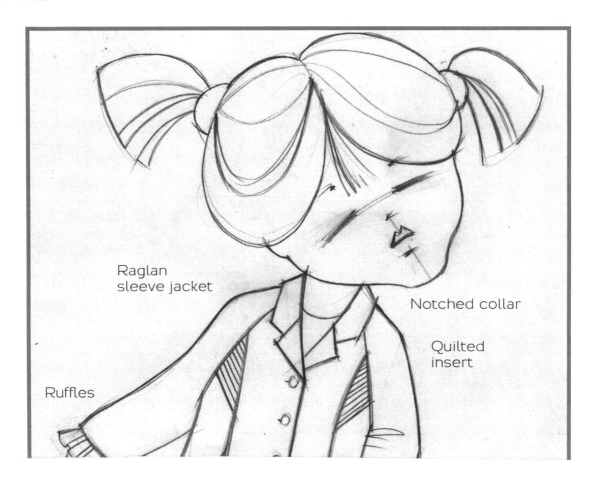

Raglan
sleeve jacket

Notched collar

Quilted
insert

Ruffles

Knife pleated
skirt

SKETCH IS CREATED
BASED ON CROQUIS
EVA (SEE PAGE 42)

(SEE PAGE 42)

Children's Wear Fashion Illustration Resource Book by Irina V. Ivanova

CHAPTER 2

Chapter 3

Styles Erica and Eric

Drawing children's figure
4 - 6 years old

Resource Book by Irina V. Ivanova

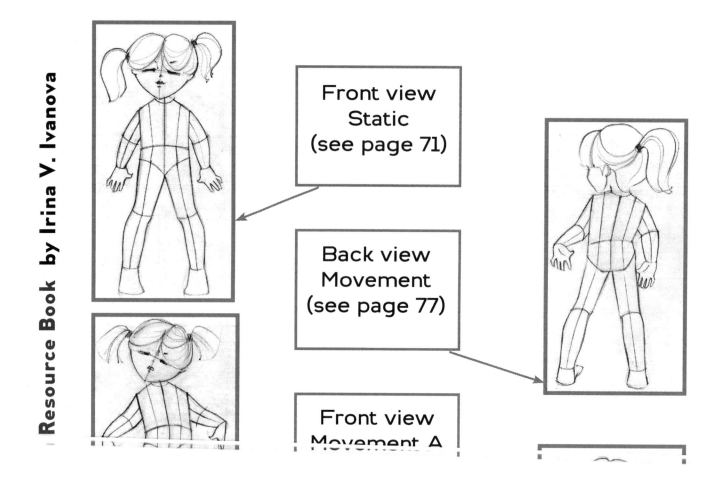

Front view
Static
(see page 71)

Back view
Movement
(see page 77)

Front view
Movement A

Children's Wear Fashion

CHAPTER 3

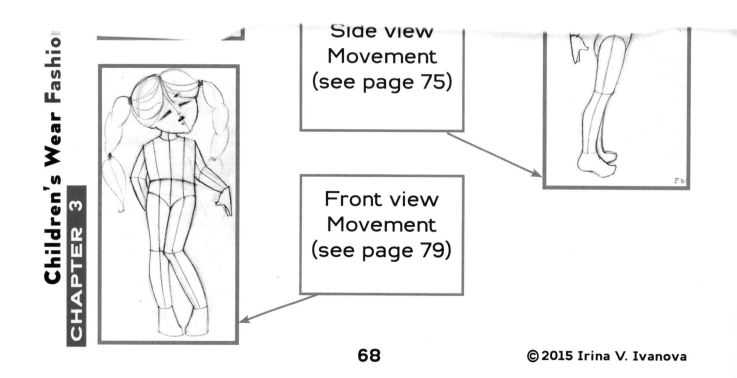

Side view
Movement
(see page 75)

Front view
Movement
(see page 79)

Boys 4-6 Years Old

Eric

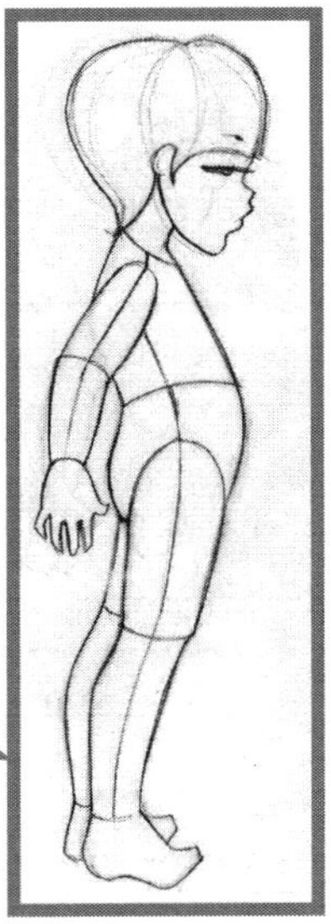

Side view
Static
(see page 70)

Front view
Movement A
(see age 72)

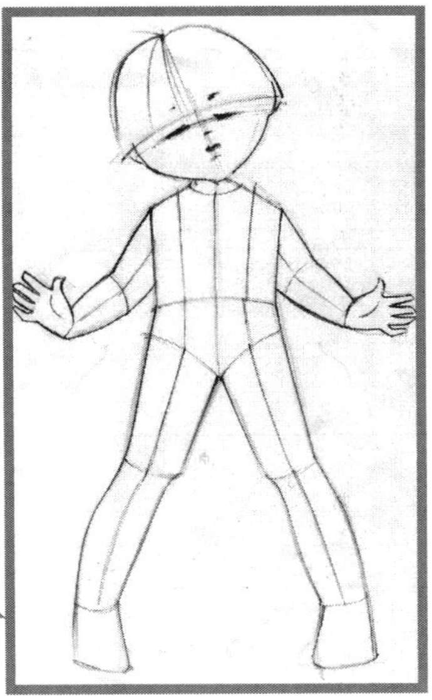

Front view
Movement B
(see page 74)

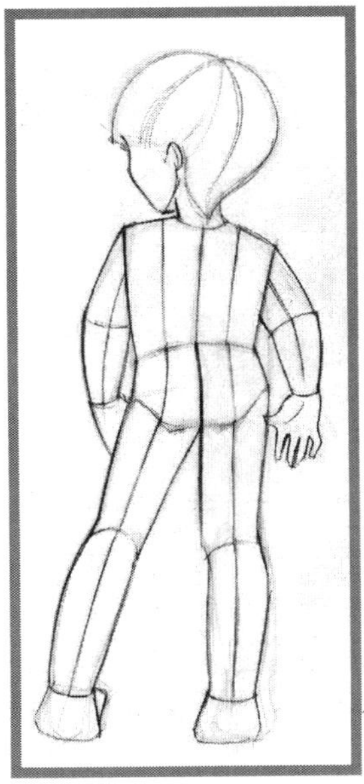

Back view
Movement
(see page 76)

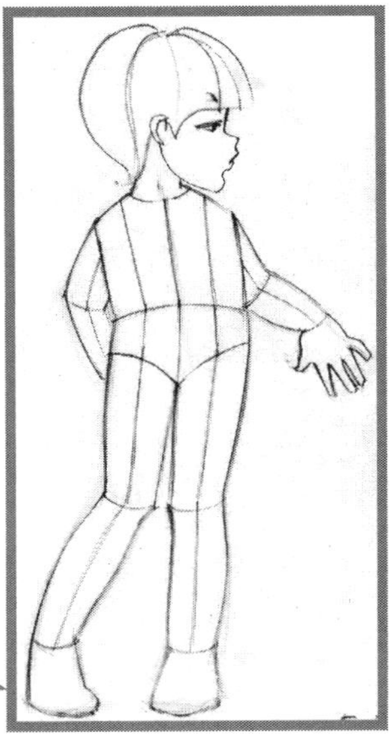

Front view
Movement C
(see page 78)

Eric

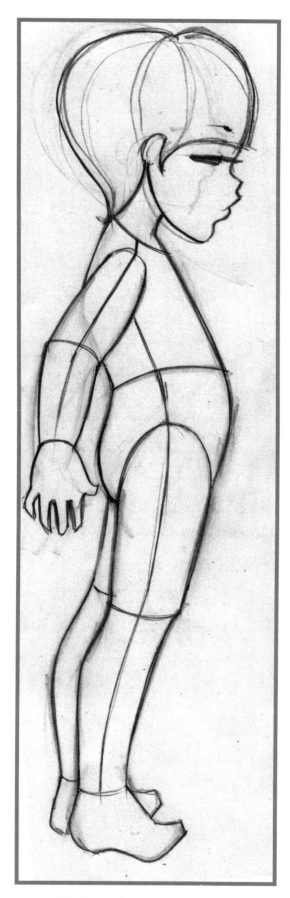

Side view. Static

Erica

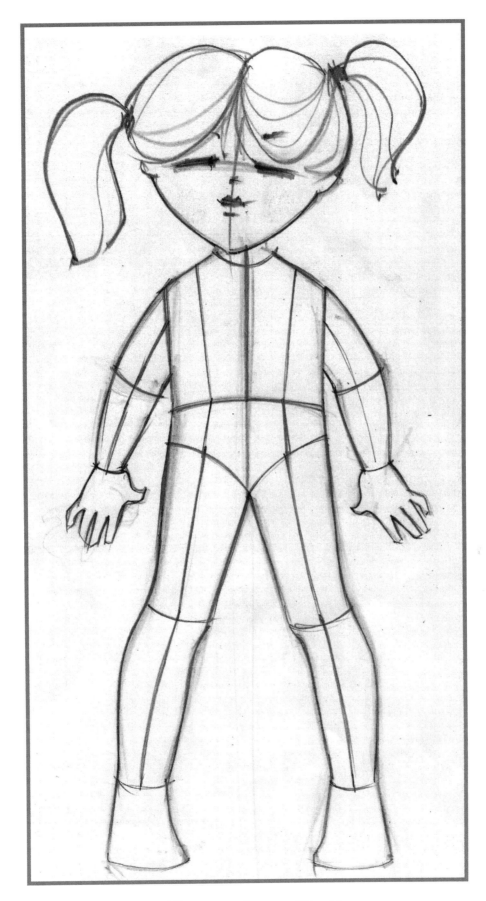

Front view. Static

71

Eric

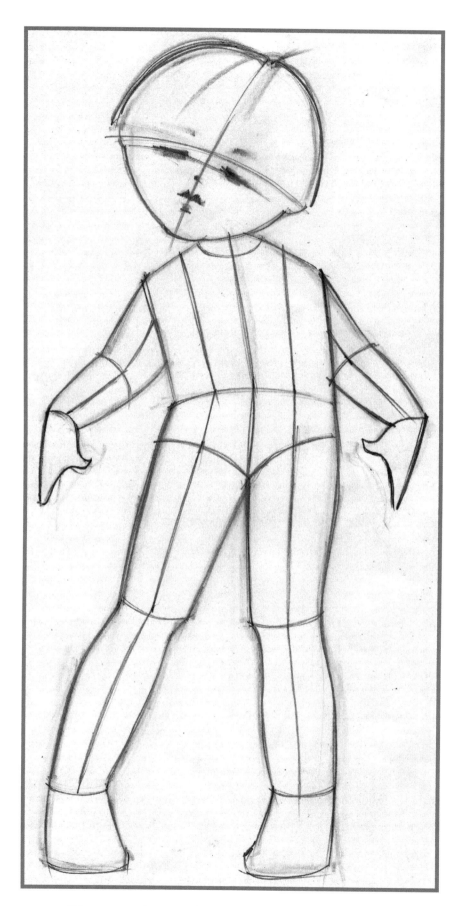

Front view. Movement A

72

Erica

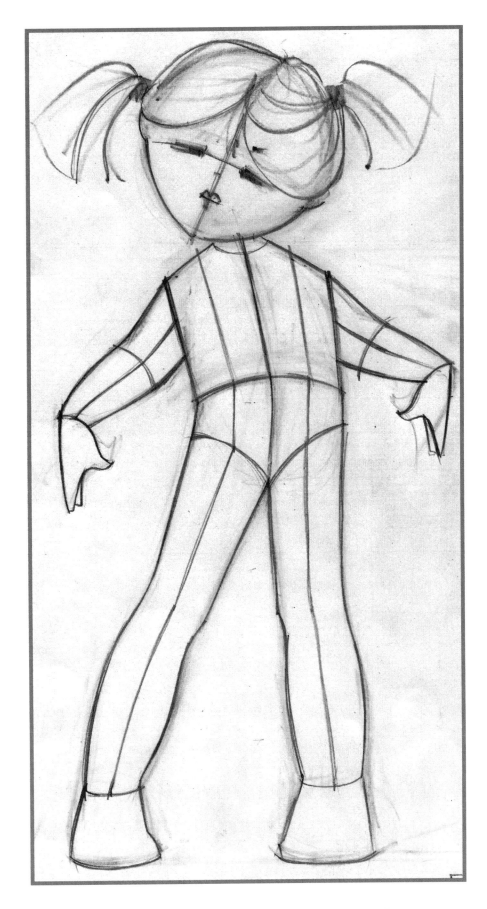

Front view. Movement A

Eric

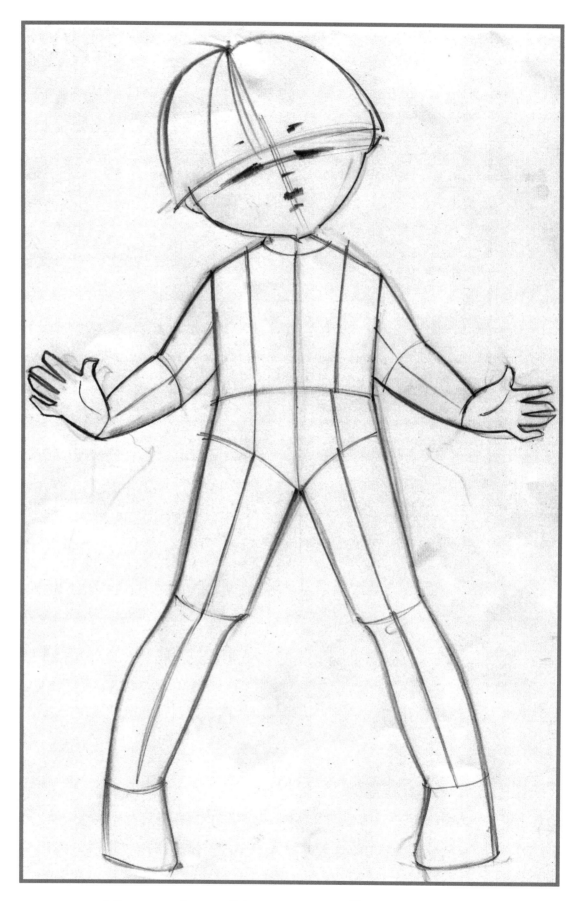

Front view. Movement B

Side view. Movement

Eric

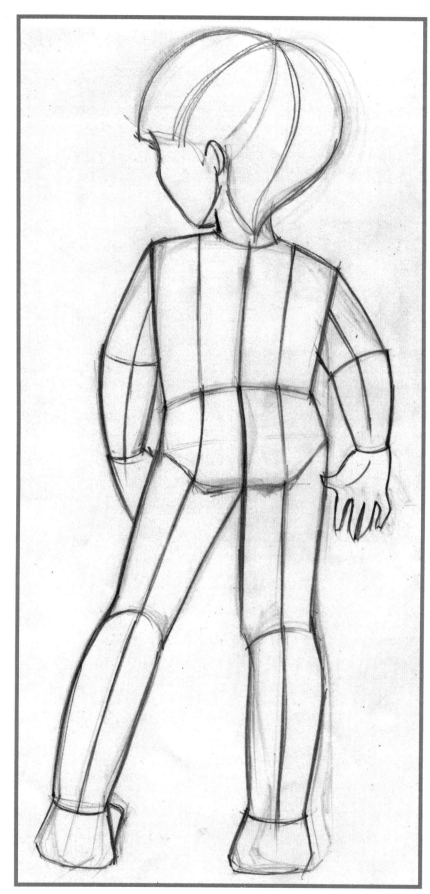

Back view. Movement

Back view. Movement

Children's Wear Fashion Illustration Resource Book by Irina V. Ivanova

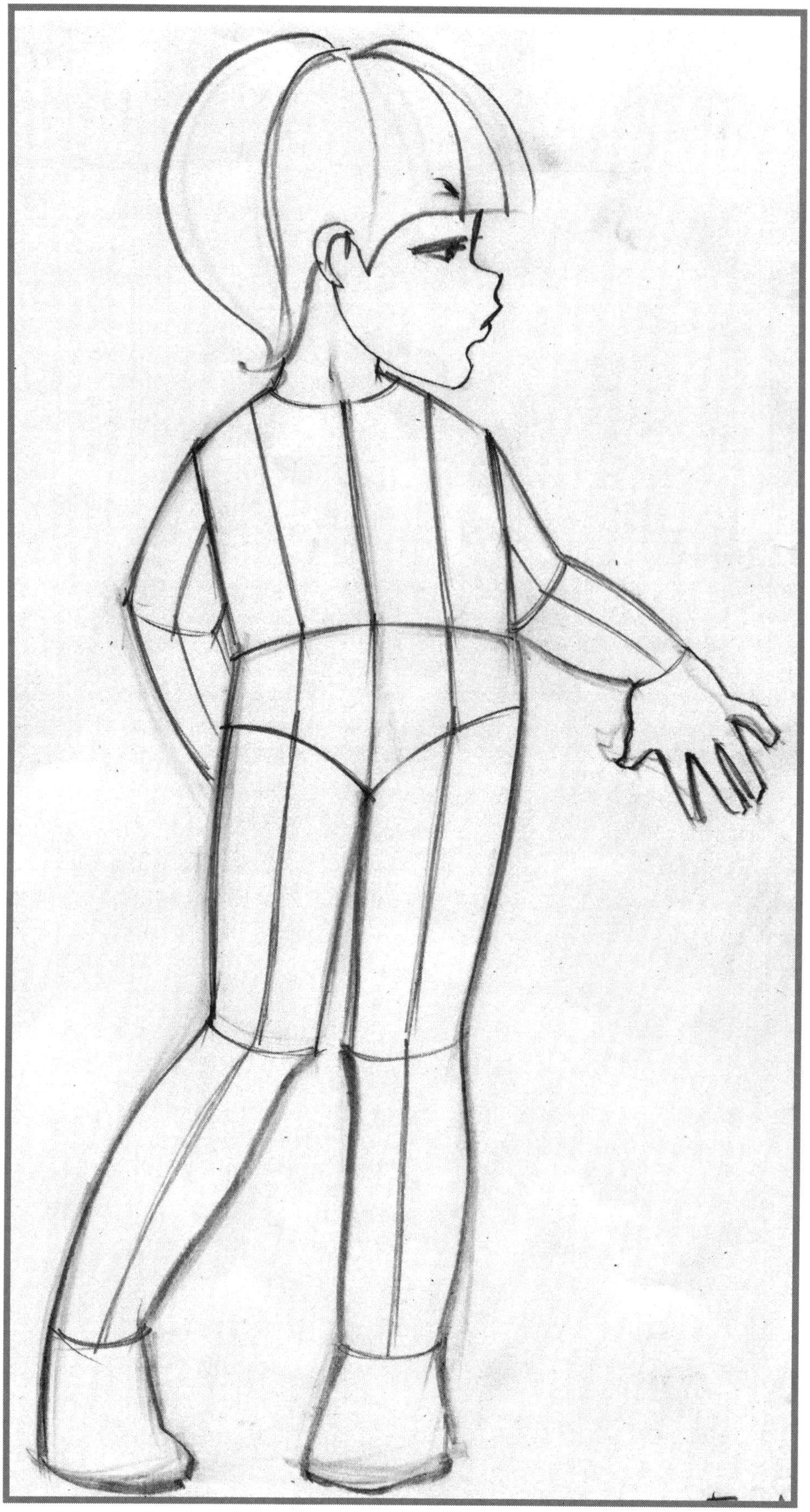

CHAPTER 3

Front view. Movement C

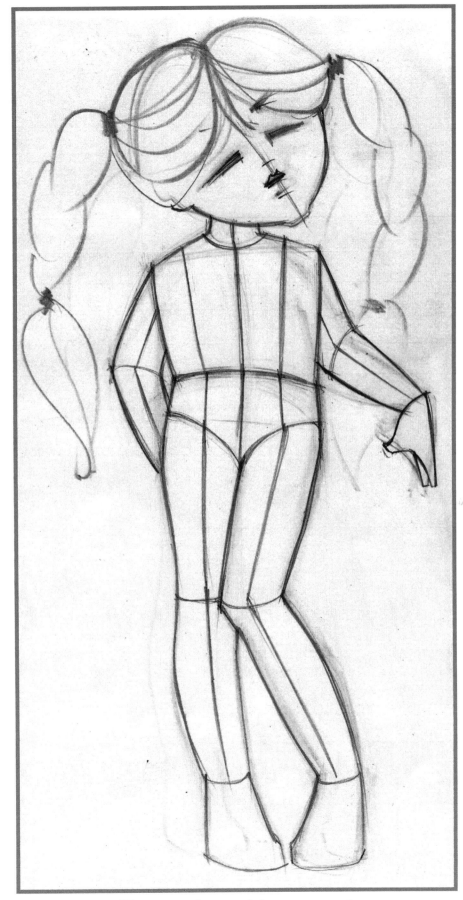

Front view. Movement

79

Eric

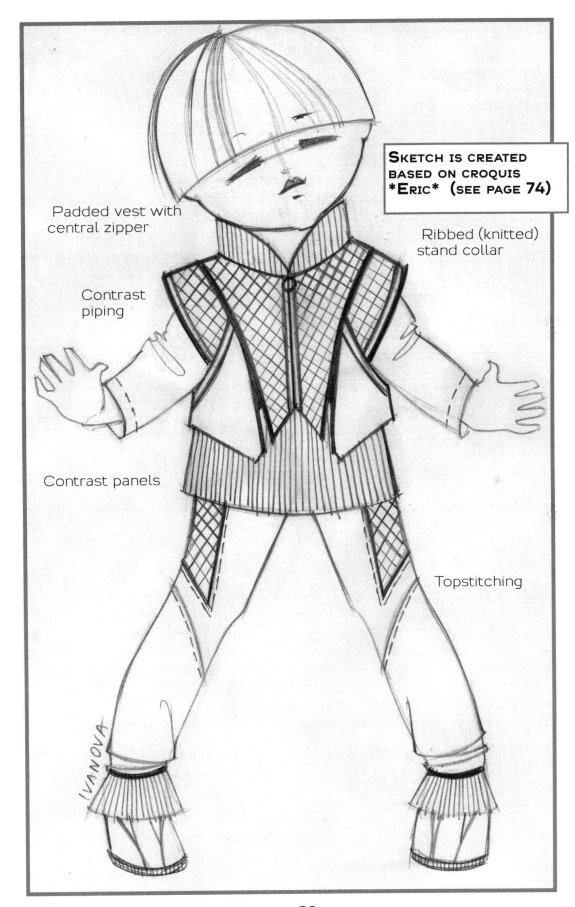

Padded vest with central zipper

Contrast piping

Contrast panels

SKETCH IS CREATED BASED ON CROQUIS *ERIC* (SEE PAGE 74)

Ribbed (knitted) stand collar

Topstitching

IVANOVA

Eric

SKETCH IS CREATED BASED ON CROQUIS *ERIC* (SEE PAGES 74 AND 78)

Children's Wear Fashion Illustration Resource Book by Irina V. Ivanova

CHAPTER 3

82

Eric

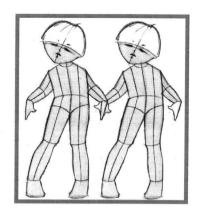

SKETCH IS CREATED BASED ON CROQUIS *ERIC* (SEE PAGE 72)

83

Erica

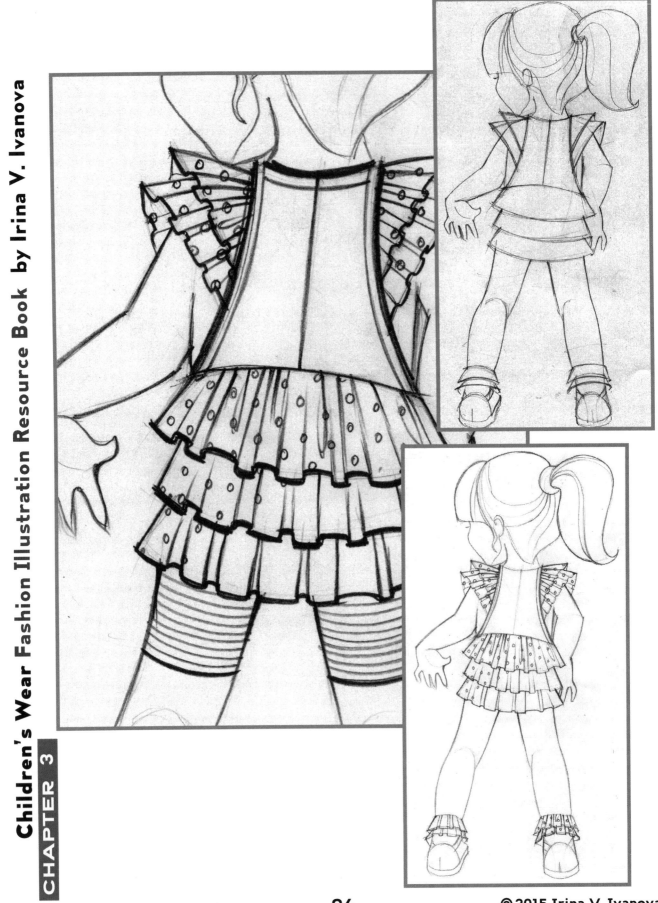

Children's Wear Fashion Illustration Resource Book by Irina V. Ivanova

CHAPTER 3

84

Erica

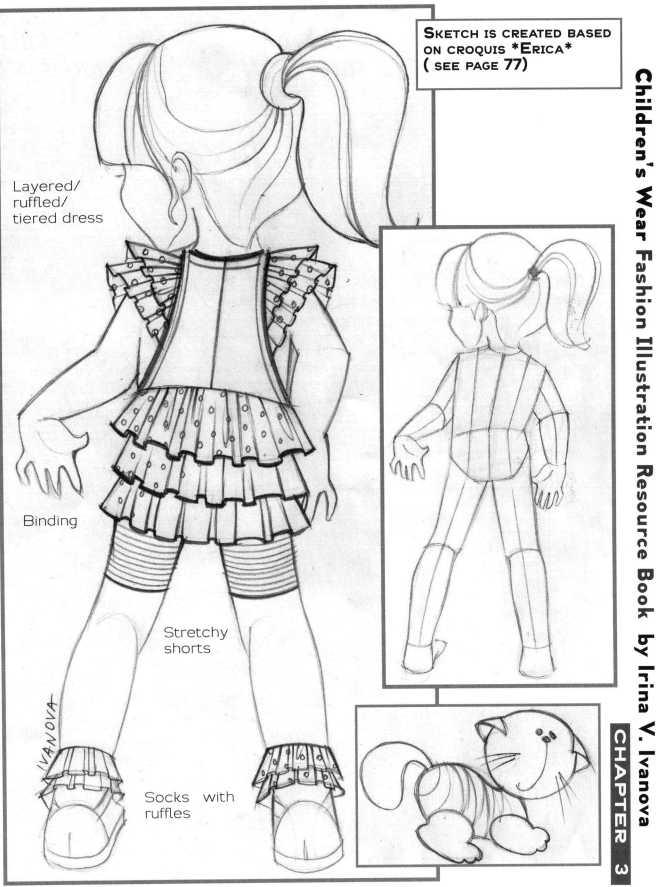

SKETCH IS CREATED BASED ON CROQUIS *ERICA* (SEE PAGE 77)

Layered/ ruffled/ tiered dress

Binding

Stretchy shorts

Socks with ruffles

IVANOVA

Children's Wear Fashion Illustration Resource Book by Irina V. Ivanova

CHAPTER 3

Erica

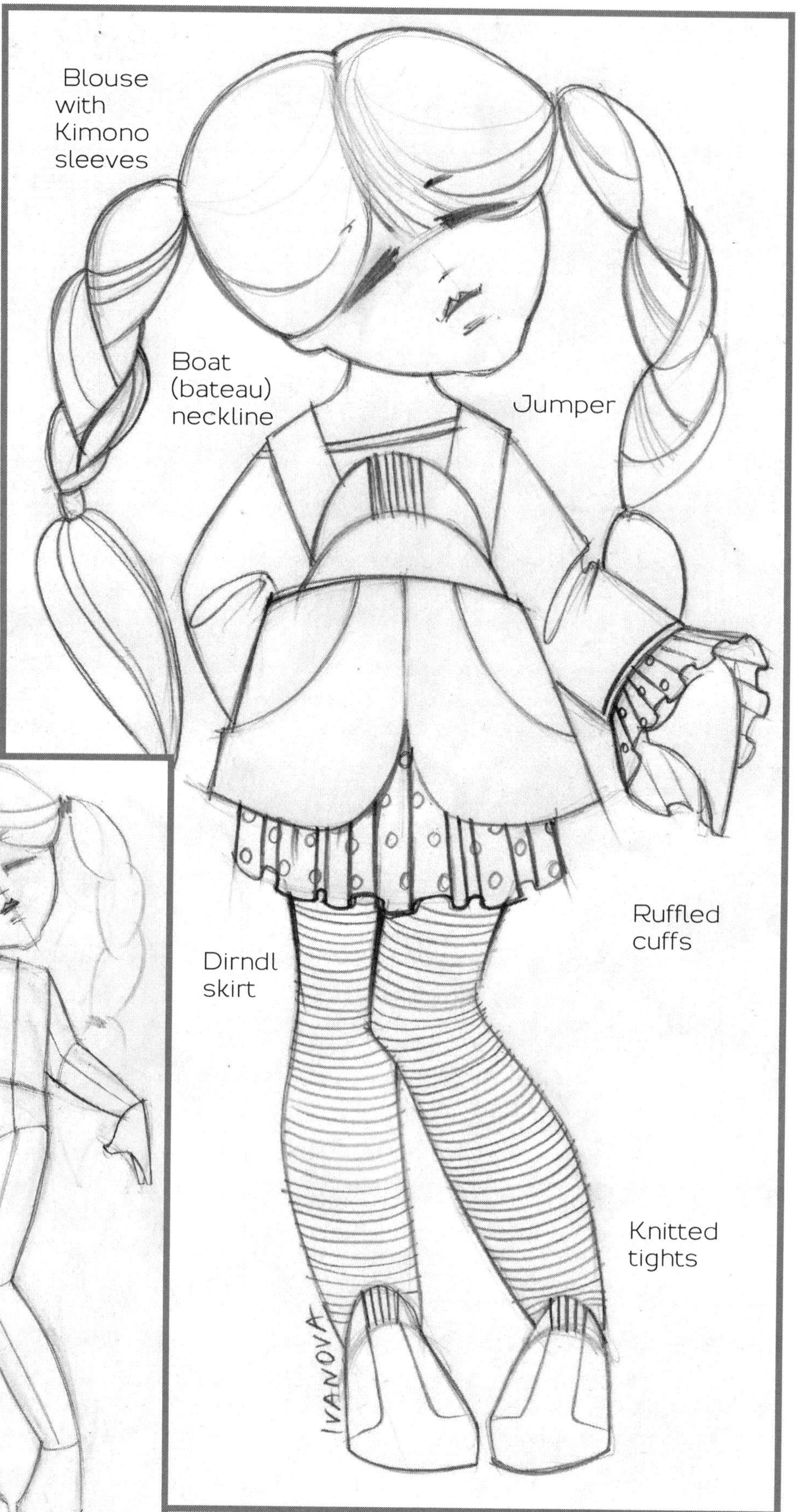

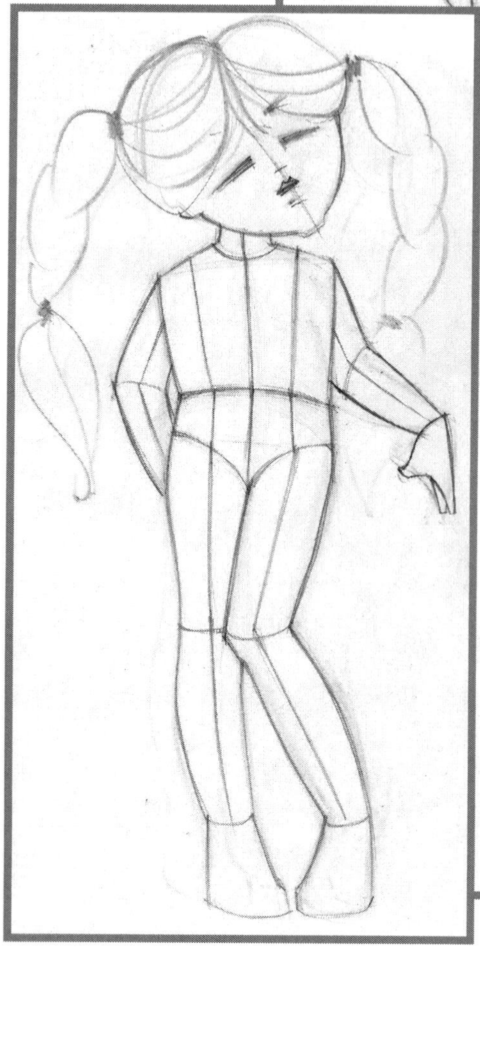

Blouse with Kimono sleeves

Boat (bateau) neckline

Jumper

Dirndl skirt

Ruffled cuffs

Knitted tights

Erica

SKETCH IS CREATED BASED ON CROQUIS *ERICA* (SEE PAGE 79)

Erica

Erica

A-line dress

Button closure

Ruffles

Knitted tights

Shoes with ruffle trim

IVANOVA

Children's Wear Fashion Illustration Resource Book by Irina V. Ivanova

Erica

Erica

Children's Wear Fashion Illustration Resource Book by Irina V. Ivanova

CHAPTER 3

© 2015 Irina V. Ivanova

Eric

Jacket with hood

Sleeves with decorative patches

On-seam pocket

Pants with decorative patches

SKETCH IS CREATED BASED ON CROQUIS *ERIC* (SEE PAGE 70)

IVANOVA

94

Single breasted coat with raglan sleeves

Flat (Puritan style) collar

Patch pockets from contract fabric

IVANOVA

SKETCH IS CREATED BASED ON CROQUIS *ERICA* (SEE PAGE 73)

Children's Wear Fashion Illustration Resource Book by Irina V. Ivanova

CHAPTER 3

Chapter 4

Styles Jessica and Jess
Drawing children's figure 7-10 years old

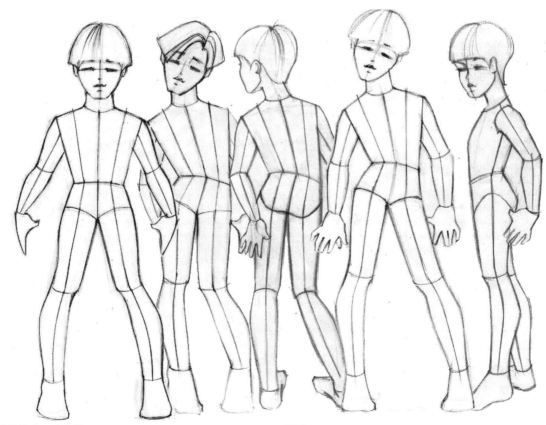

97

Jessica

Girls 7-10 Years Old

Children's Wear Fashion Illustration Resource Book by Irina V. Ivanova

CHAPTER 4

Front view
Movement A
(see page 100)

Front view
Static
(see page 102)

Front view
Movement B
(see page 106)

Back view
Movement
(see page 104)

Side view
Movement
(see page 108)

Boys 7-10 Years Old

Jess

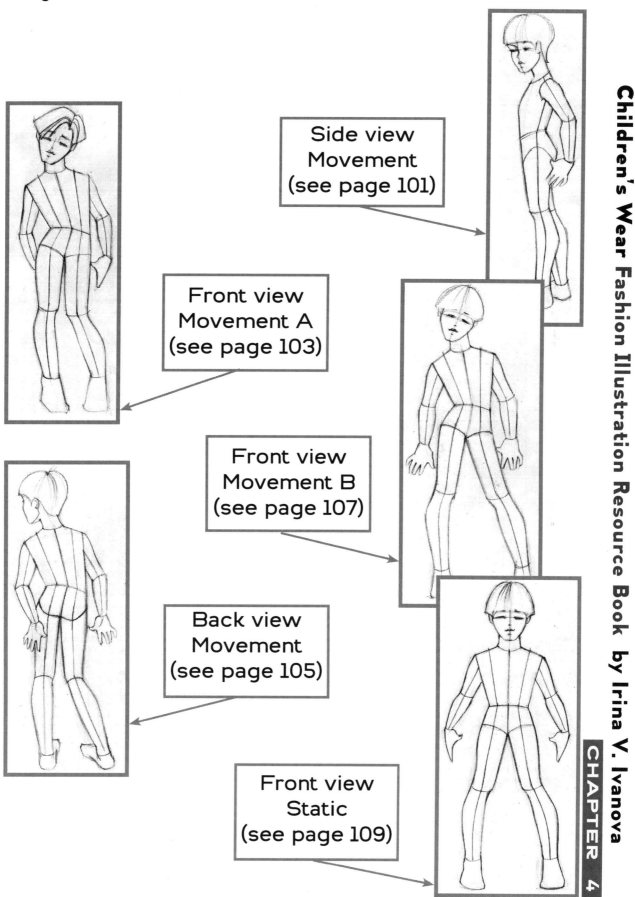

Side view
Movement
(see page 101)

Front view
Movement A
(see page 103)

Front view
Movement B
(see page 107)

Back view
Movement
(see page 105)

Front view
Static
(see page 109)

Children's Wear Fashion Illustration Resource Book by Irina V. Ivanova

CHAPTER 4

Jessica

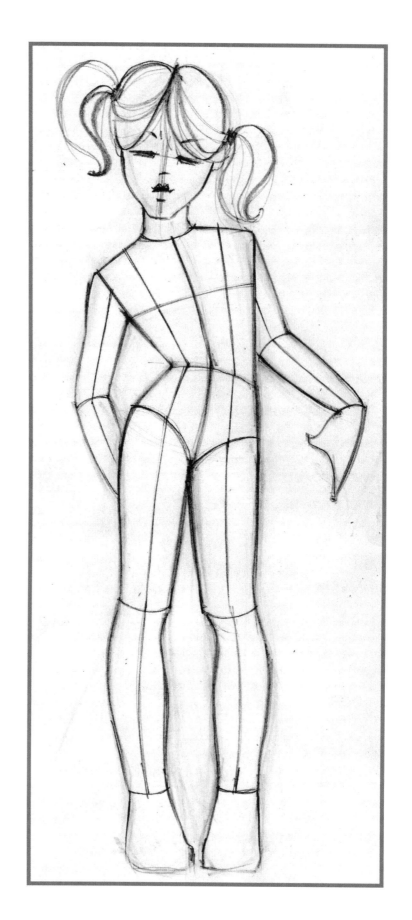

Front view. Movement A

100

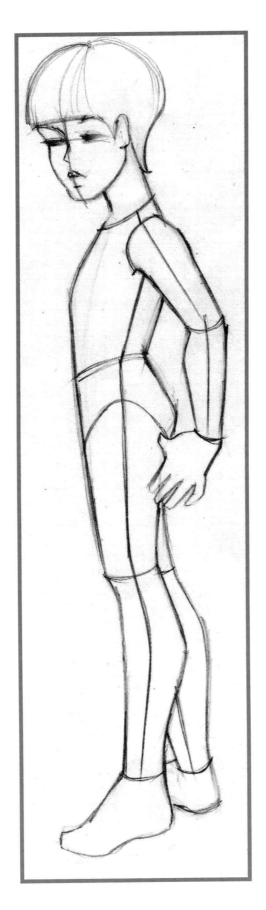

Side view. Movement

Jessica

Children's Wear Fashion Illustration Resource Book by Irina V. Ivanova

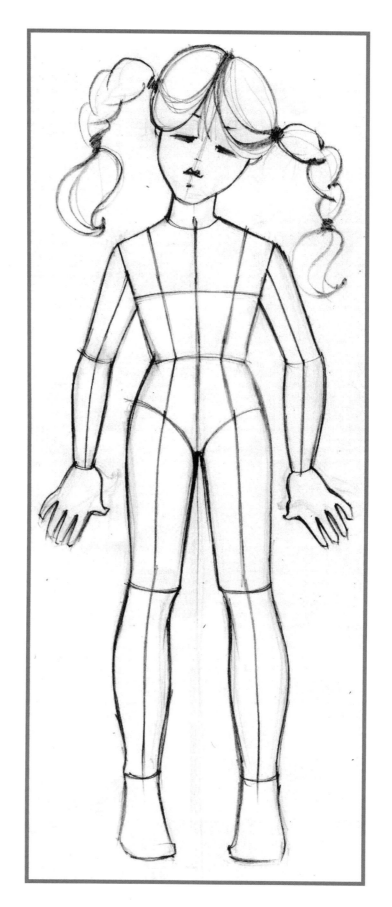

Front view. Static

102

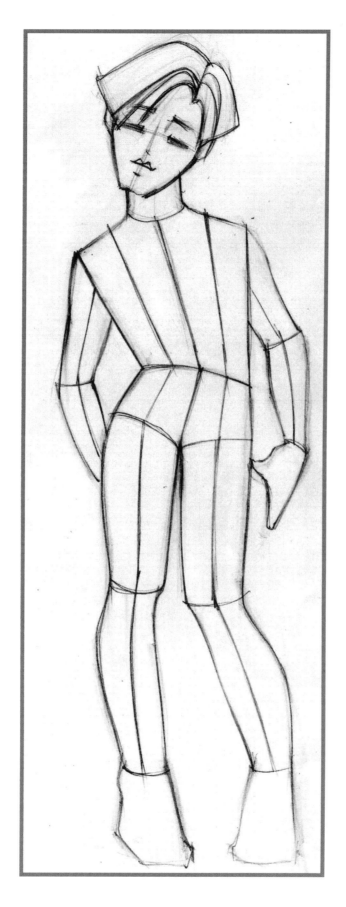

Front view. Movement A

Children's Wear Fashion Illustration Resource Book by Irina V. Ivanova

CHAPTER 4

Jessica

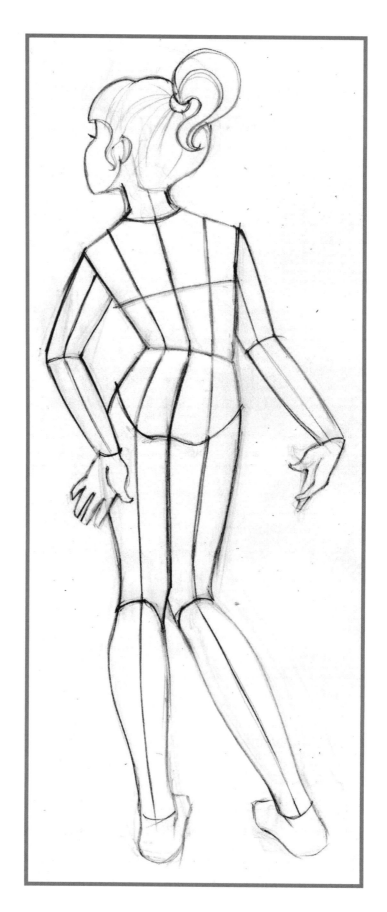

Back view. Movement

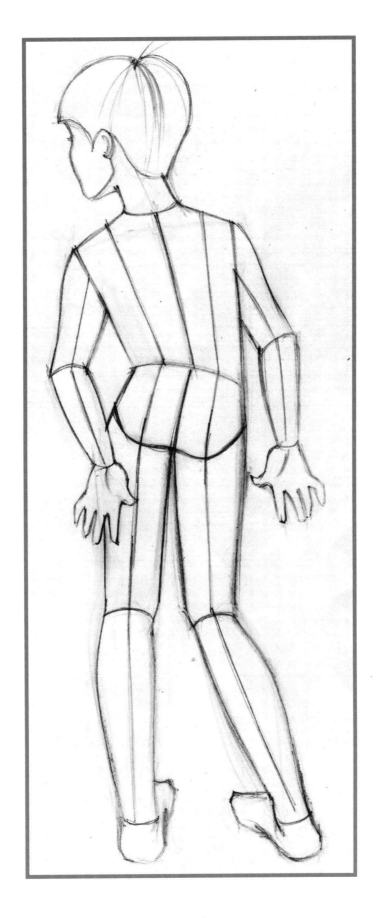

Back view. Movement

Children's Wear Fashion Illustration Resource Book by Irina V. Ivanova

CHAPTER 4

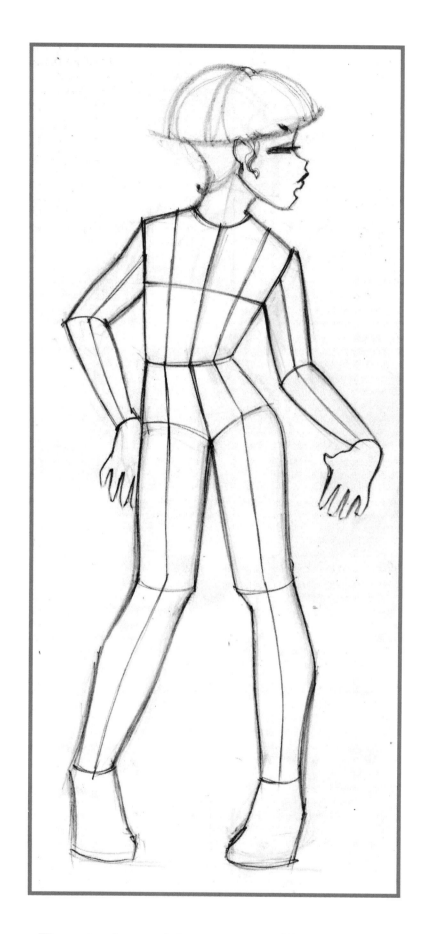

Front view. Movement B

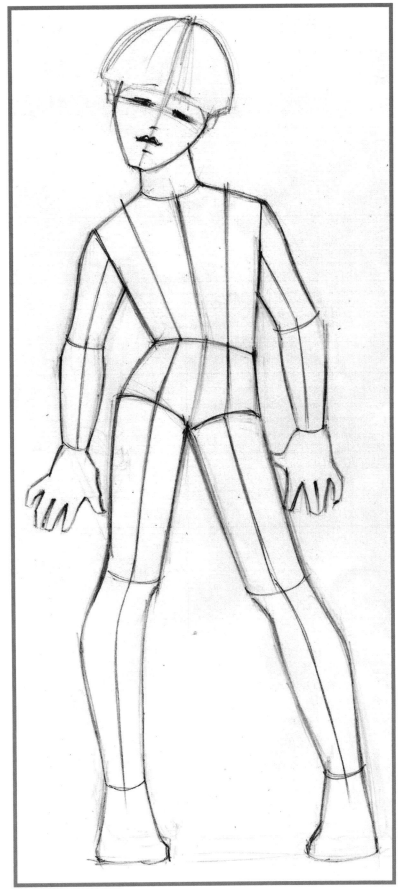

Front view. Movement B

Jessica

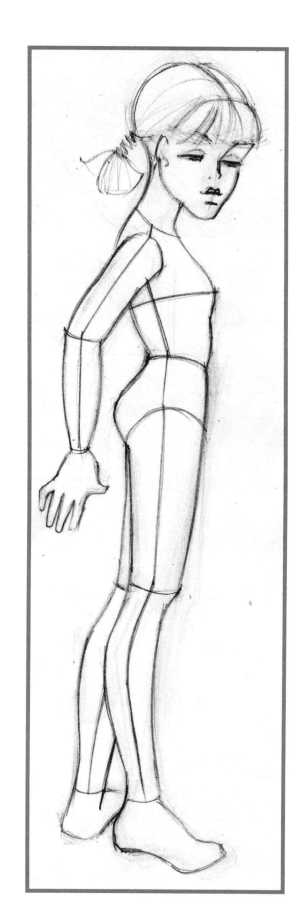

Side view. Movement

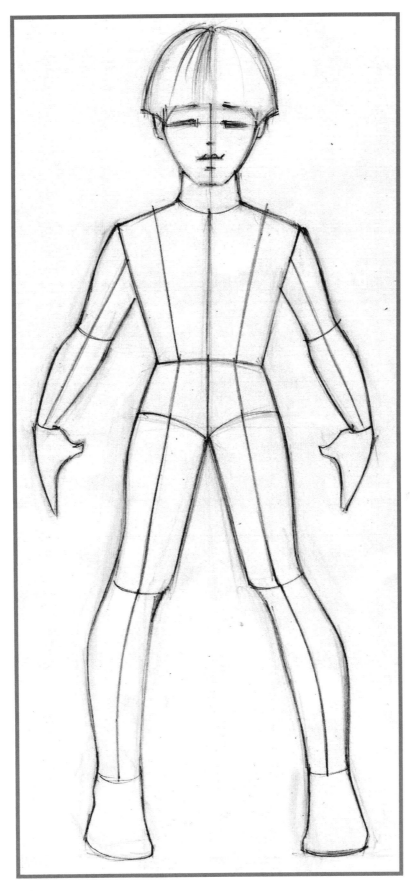

Front view. Static

Children's Wear Fashion Illustration Resource Book by Irina V. Ivanova

Jess

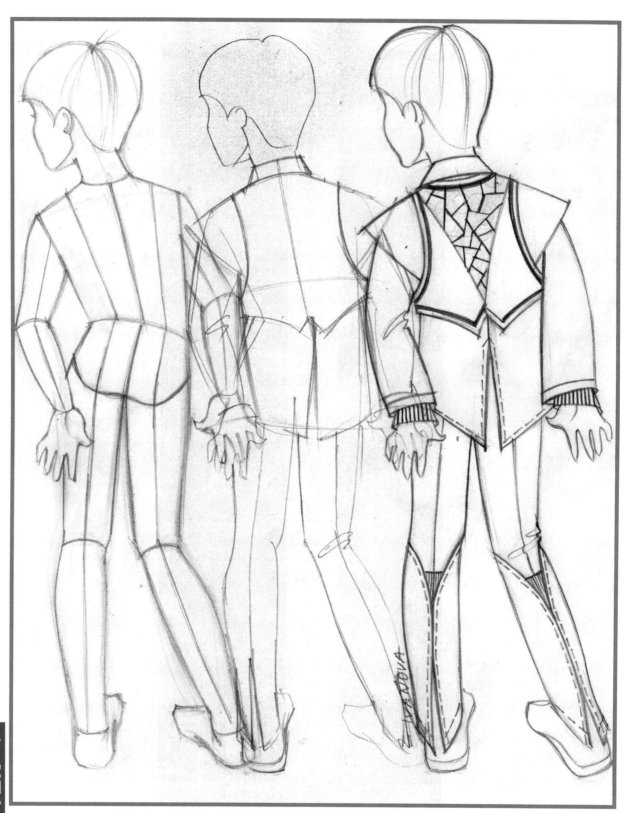

Jess

Vest with hood and central zipper

Pants with decorative patches

IVANOVA

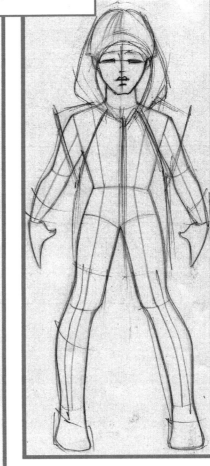

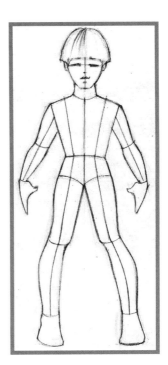

Children's Wear Fashion Illustration Resource Book   by Irina V. Ivanova

CHAPTER 4

Jess

SKETCH IS CREATED BASED ON CROQUIS *JESS* (SEE PAGE 101)

Jess

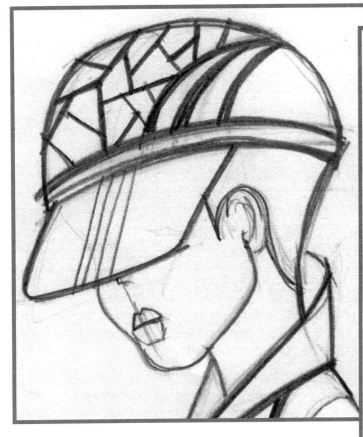

Cap

Vest with stand collar

Decorative inserts on cap, pants, and vest

Rolled up shirt set–in sleeve

113

Jessica and Jess

Children's Wear Fashion Illustration Resource Book by Irina V. Ivanova

Jessica and Jess

SKETCH IS CREATED BASED ON CROQUIS *JESS* (SEE PAGE 103) AND *JESSICA* (SEE PAGE 106)

Children's Wear Fashion Illustration Resource Book by Irina V. Ivanova

CHAPTER 4

Jess

Vest with double
breasted closure

Shirt with hidden
closure

Children's Wear Fashion Illustration Resource Book   by Irina V. Ivanova

SKETCH IS CREATED BASED
ON CROQUIS *JESS*
(SEE PAGE 107)

Jessica

118

SKETCH IS CREATED BASED ON
CROQUIS *JESSICA*
(SEE PAGES 108, 100, 102)

Jessica

Sleeveless top with lacing on the back

Contrast binding

Draped skirt and shorts with asymmetrical ruffles attached

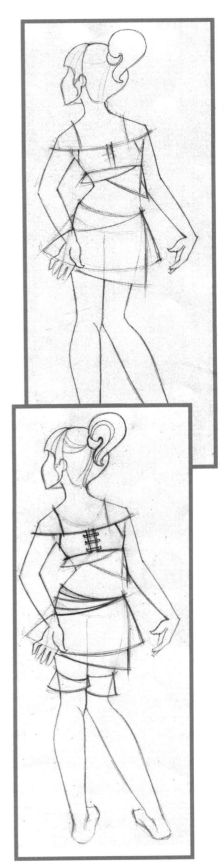

120

Jessica

SKETCH IS CREATED BASED ON CROQUIS *JESSICA* (SEE PAGE 104)

Children's Wear Fashion Illustration Resource Book by Irina V. Ivanova

CHAPTER 4

Jessica

SKETCH IS CREATED BASED ON CROQUIS *JESSICA* (SEE PAGE 108)

Wide brimmed hat without crown

Halter neckline

Knitted shorts with ruffles attached

IVANOVA

Jessica

Draped top and skirt with asymmetrical ruffles

SKETCH IS CREATED BASED ON CROQUIS *JESSICA* (SEE PAGE 102)

SEE PAGE 102

Children's Wear Fashion Illustration Resource Book by Irina V. Ivanova

CHAPTER 4

Jessica

SKETCH IS CREATED BASED ON CROQUIS *JESSICA* (SEE PAGE 100)

Draped top and skirt with asymmetrical ruffles attached

Children's Wear Fashion Illustration Resource Book by Irina V. Ivanova

CHAPTER 4

124

BOOK SUMMARY

On the pages 128–129, you can see all templates placed together for a better visual understanding of differences in proportions between children of different age groups. The size of each template needs to be adjusted according to its own age group when templates for different age groups are drawn together in one illustration.

For example, when drawing children of 2–3 years old side by side with children of 6–7 years old, the templates for younger children must be reduced in size in comparison with templates for older children (please see images below).

incorrect   correct

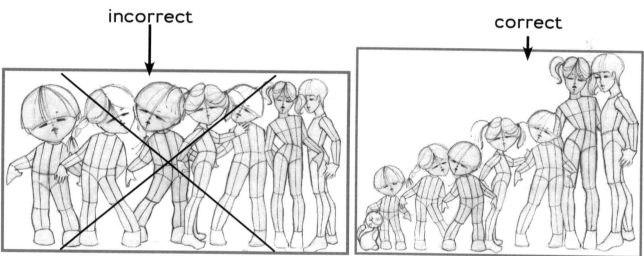

BASIC REVIEW OF CHILDREN'S PROPORTIONS

Traditionally, proportions of the human body in fashion illustrations are always given by "head count" using head size as a measuring unit. Anatomically correct proportions for an average adult is 7–8 heads. However, in fashion illustration the "head count" is very approximate and is intentionally exaggerated. For example, 9 heads is a commonly accepted standard for an illustrating adult figure.

Proportions of children's figures presented in the book are stylized as well. For children's fashion illustration, there cannot be one standard due to variations in age. In other words, the standard depends on the age of a child. Even inside one age group there is a lot of room for flexibility. In real life children of the same age can have visibly different proportions of the body.

Children's Wear Fashion Illustration Resource Book by Irina V. Ivanova

ALEX STYLE

(0-1 years old babies) croquis has approximately 3 heads in body length.

- The shape of the head and the body is very rounded.

- The neck is very short, almost unseen, so it could be proportionally ignored.

- There is no distinctive waistline in baby's body, but tummies are very protruded.

- The arms and legs are very short and hands and feet are round in shape.

- There is no difference in the proportion of girls and boys yet in this age.

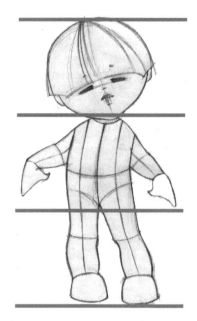

3 heads proportions

EVA AND EVAN STYLE

(1-3 years old kids) croquis has about 3,5-4 heads in body length.

- Still there is no big difference between boys and girls in proportions of the body and head shape.

- The legs and arms are a little longer and skinnier.

- The neck is very short.

- The shape of the head is still round and faces are very small in proportion to the size of the head.

3,5 heads proportions

4 heads proportions

ERICA AND ERIC STYLE

(4-6 years old kids) croquis has about 4-5 heads in body length.

- Very small difference between proportions for girls and boys.

- The shape of the heads are still rounded, but faces are longer.

- The neck is longer and waistline is slightly noticeable.

- The body loses their roundness and puffiness.

JESSICA AND JESS STYLE

(7-10 years old kids) croquis has roughly 5-6 heads lengths in body length.

- The shape of the head is close to an oval, so it has no round shape anymore.

- Faces are longer and hairline is higher.

- In children of this age, we can see the difference in proportions of girls and boys.

- Boys are more masculine in the shape of the body, arms, and legs. They have heavier face line and stronger shoulders and necks.

- Girls of this age group have more contrast between waistline and shoulders. They have a more curved shoulder line and lighter face bones.

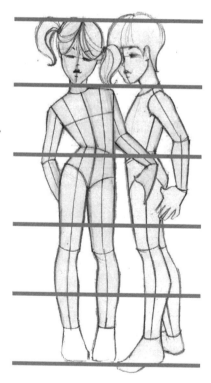

5 heads proportions

Please note that all drawings are stylized for very general guidance and direction and should be adjusted if needed with designer's own discretion. Templates in the book are meant to reflect the logic of a fashion drawing process and no intention to have "scientifically correct" proportions of children's figure.

Figure drawing templates for children's wear by Irina V. Ivanova

Alex Age group 0-1 years old **Alex**

Evan Age group 1-3 years old **Eva**

Eric Age group 4-6 years old **Erica**

Jess Age group 7-10 years old **Jessica**

Children's Wear Fashion Illustration Resource Book by Irina V. Ivanova

Alex   Age group 0-1 years old   **Alex**

Evan   Age group 1-3 years old   **Eva**

Eric   Age group 4-6 years old   **Erica**

Jess   Age group 7-10 years old   **Jessica**

Children's Wear Fashion Illustration Resource Book by Irina V. Ivanova

We wish you happy drawing!
Enjoy your children's wear projects!!!

Please share your feedback on the book
at:
contact@artdesignproject.com

About the author: professional visual artist and illustrator Irina V. Ivanova is a fashion designer by training, experience and passion.

Irina's previous publications include two figure drawing template books for fashion illustration: "Figure Drawing Templates Set 1: Standard Woman's Figure" and "Figure Drawing Templates Set 2: Standard Man's Figure."

Irina's third book benefits from her practical experience as a fashion designer, from her mastery in visual arts, as well as from years of her teaching college level fashion design courses.

When not creating her books Irina is working on her visual art projects by painting and drawing in her Hallandale Beach, Florida art studio.

On this page you can see some   of Irina's fashion illustrations from her *Ruff Couture* collection of drawings.

Children's Wear Fashion Illustration Resource Book is a practical aid for fashion drawing. There are 40 figure drawing templates for 4 different age groups, complemented with multiple sketches and illustrations. All figures are shown in front, back, three-quarter and side views.

The book is very visual – you can see the main steps of the drawing process for each illustration.

There is no text in the book other than captions, a short introduction and a brief summary. The book is designed to be a visual aid for fashion illustration of children's wear. Figure templates, raw sketches and accomplished fashion illustration is the main content of the book.

The book is very instructive and practical. Sketches are created from the templates and turned into finished illustrations. All drawings are made with simple pencil only. Roughness and sketchiness of these drawings is carefully preserved. Trace a template from the book and draw fashion sketches with the template. Fashion sketching with the book is less stressful and tends to smooth the designer's workflow.

Drawing children's fashion illustration becomes fun and accurate when using Children's Wear Fashion Illustration Resource Book.